TALES OF DORSET

By Linda Fernley

BRADWELL
BOOKS

Published by Bradwell Books

9 Orgreave Close Sheffield S13 9NP

Email: books@bradwellbooks.co.uk

British Library Cataloguing in Publication Data: a
catalogue record for this book is available from the British

1st Edition

ISBN: 9781910551301

Print: Gomer Press, Llandysul, Ceredigion SA44 4JL

Design by: Andrew Caffrey

Typeset by: Mark Titterton

Photograph Credits: Linda Fernley, Creative Commons,
others credited individually and where indicated iStock

INTRODUCTION

Covering an area of 1,024 square miles (2,653 sq km), Dorset borders Devon to the west, Somerset to the north-west, Wiltshire to the north-east and Hampshire to the east. The county town is Dorchester, and after the reorganisation of local government in 1974 the county's border was extended eastward to include the Hampshire towns of Bournemouth and Christchurch. The population is approximately 750,000, half of whom live in the South East Dorset conurbation, while the rest of the county is largely rural with a low population density.

For further factual information on the county's geography or history, or to discover which well-known places you should visit and why, may I politely invite you to head for the enormous amount of excellent tourist guide books and local history volumes – expertly researched and complied by scholars and serious travel writers – which you will surely find in any good library or book shop.

No, it's not our purpose here to share with you the recognised facts about Dorset.

Instead, for these Tales and Trivia books we've delighted in rummaging about to seek out the more peculiar, funny, off-the-wall or lesser known tit-bits about the county's people, places, objects, customs and history. We hope that these morsels will not only add to your enjoyment of Dorset but will also surprise, entertain or flabbergast you … or at least give you something to talk about when you next find yourself lost for words!

So from dinosaurs to silkworms, from chillies to giants, from UFOs to granny's teeth, these pages will show you a Dorset crying out to be explored from a different angle. You don't have to read the book sequentially from beginning to end – just dip in and out as the fancy takes you … and happy reading!

PUTTING DORSET ON THE MAP

The first UFO ever to be spotted in British skies was recorded on 8 December 1733 in Fleet, Dorset. James Cracker was standing in a valley in broad daylight when he saw 'something in the sky which appeared in the north but vanished from my sight, as it was intercepted by trees … on a sudden it re-appeared, darting in and out of my sight with an amazing coruscation. The colour of this phenomenon was like burnished, or new washed silver. It shot with speed like a star falling in the night.' The next day it was discovered that a Mr Edgecombe and another gentleman had witnessed the same phenomenon at precisely the same time, about 15 miles from where James had seen it, going from east to north. The sighting preceded the term 'UFO' by over 200 years.

Abbotsbury Swannery is the only managed colony of nesting mute swans in the world, and likely the oldest farmed herd or flock in the country. Records trace the existence of the swannery back to 1393, but as the abbey it belonged to was established in 1040, it probably existed from nearer that date. Benedictine monks farmed the swans as a source of meat for their lavish banquets. In 1539, the abbey was dissolved by King Henry VIII and then bought by Sir Giles Strangways, whose family has owned it for 15 generations and still run it today. The swannery, which has approximately 600 swans, has become a tourist attraction and is the only place in the world where visitors can walk through the heart of a colony of nesting mute swans. Swans are normally very territorial birds but the Abbotsbury swans have become used to visitors and allow them to approach, even in the nesting season. An Abbotsbury swan was used by Jacob Epstein as a model for St Michael's wings on his sculpture of the saint's victory over the devil at Coventry Cathedral.

Abbotsbury
Swannery
iStock

Mary Anning (1799–1847) opened **Britain's first fossil shop** in her hometown of Lyme Regis, West Dorset in 1826. Mary's family had long supplemented their modest income by salvaging fossils from the cliffs and selling them as souvenirs to holidaymakers. The town had become a popular seaside resort by the late 1700s, and fossil-collecting was a fashionable activity – first as a hobby, and later as a science as it was discovered that fossils contained important clues to understanding both geology and biology.

Mary's father, Richard, often took her and her brother along on his fossil hunts to make more money for the family. It was dangerous work, since it was during the winter, when rain caused landslides, that new fossils were revealed and collectors were most tempted to go exploring. Sadly Richard Anning died in 1810, aged 44, from injuries and tuberculosis following a fall from one of the cliffs.

Undeterred, Mary followed in the family footsteps and became famous for the important finds she made in the Blue Lias cliffs around Lyme Regis, one of the richest fossil locations in the country. When she was just 12, she and her brother unearthed an ichthyosaur skeleton, which was sold to a collector for £23 and displayed in London.

Ichthyosaur
skeleton
Creative Commons

By 1825, Mary had taken the lead in the family business. She soon became an expert in the field, and made key contributions to scientific thinking about prehistoric life and the history of the planet. She was consulted by academics, and even visited by King Frederick Augustus II of Saxony. Nevertheless, as a woman, she was not eligible to join the Geological Society of London. In 2010, 163 years after her death, the Royal Society named her as one of the ten most influential British women in the history of science.

Even if you've never heard of Mary Anning, you're sure to know the tongue twister that was written in 1908 and directly inspired by her life story:

She sells seashells on the seashore
The shells she sells are seashells I'm sure
So if she sells seashells on the seashore
Then I'm sure she sells seashore shells.

(original text written in 1908 by Terry Sullivan, set to music by Harry Gifford)

The **Jurassic Coast** was the first natural site in England to make it onto the UNESCO World Heritage List, an honour it received for the variety of geological periods it represents. It covers 95 miles (155km) from Orcombe Point in East Devon to Old Harry Rocks in Dorset, and documents 185 million years of the Earth's history. By following the South West Coast Path, you can walk the entire length of the coast. The highest point on the Jurassic Coast, and on the entire south coast of England, is Golden Cap, which stands at 191 metres (627 feet) – it's quite a stiff climb (and I'm speaking from experience!) but well worth the effort. If you approach it from the west, rather than the east, the hike is slightly less torturous.

David Squire, town crier, has been serving Ringwood since 1958 – making him the **longest-serving town crier** ever. Town criers traditionally spread news through a town and in days gone by served as the king's spokesmen. They were highly regarded, usually people of good standing in the community, and protected by law – any harm done to a town crier was considered harm done to the king, and therefore a

David Squire,
Town Crier
Creative Commons

treasonable offence. The phrase 'The Post' to refer to newspapers came from the town crier practice of nailing official proclamations to the doorpost of the local inn after announcements had been made.

David is one of only 150 remaining town criers in the UK. He was a fifteen-year-old choirboy when he first 'cried' at the ancient Beating the Bounds ceremony. Over the years, he has appeared at thousands of civic events and charity functions, won many an award, and even represented both his town and his country in competitions. He intends to continue until he has reached the 60-year mark. His role is unpaid.

The **world's earliest radio station** was set up by Guglielmo Marconi (1874–1937), known as 'the father of wireless', on the coast of Dorset. He was born in Bologna, Italy, and as a student was captivated by 'the idea of transmitting messages through space by means of etheric waves'. The Italian government was unenthusiastic about his early experiments, so he came to London in 1896, where he put on demonstrations for an audience of scientists and the military. Marconi was convinced that wireless would offer greater benefit at sea than on land; so with his assistant George Kemp, he travelled to the Isle of Wight and set up the first ever fixed transmitting station at the Royal Needles Hotel.

Marconi with his radio equipment
Creative Commons

They began a series of experiments using tug boats belonging to the South Western Railway Company at Lymington, sailing within a triangular course – from Alum Pier to Bournemouth Pier, on to Swanage Pier and back to Alum – and noting the signal strength at different points. They erected a station at the Haven Hotel on Sandbanks in 1898, with the aim of signalling to Swanage on the west and the Isle of Wight on the east or to ships at sea. After a few initial glitches, Marconi gave successful demonstrations from the Royal Needles Hotel to the Haven Hotel on 9 January 1899, essentially inventing radio communication. The Haven Hotel has now developed into a huge modern edifice, and there is a plaque pointing out the small room that gave birth to the 'Wireless Age'.

A plaque in Melcombe, Weymouth tells of how the **Black Death** first entered Britain through this port in 1348. The Greyfriars' Chronicle, a news source of the time, said: 'Two ships, one of them from Bristol, came alongside. One of the sailors had brought with him from Gascony the seeds of the terrible pestilence and through him the men of that town of Melcombe were the first in England to be infected.' The plague had come from the Far East across Eurasia, spread by land and sea trading routes and the rats that scurried on and off the ships. From Melcombe, it soon spread to the other villages near Weymouth, and residents began to flee, helping to spread the disease even further. By the time the first wave of the Black Death died down, as the plaque notes, it had killed an incredible '30–50% of the country's total population'.

Durdle Door is a world-famous natural arch of limestone found on the coast near Lulworth, and is extremely popular with visitors. The remarkable arch was formed from softer rocks being eroded away behind the hard limestone, allowing the sea to gradually break through. The name derives from thirl, an Old English word meaning 'to bore or drill'. Unusually beautiful and set in a vast expanse of ocean, Durdle Door has served as a backdrop for several films and pop videos, from Tears for Fears' Shout of 1985 and Cliff Richard's 1990 hit Saviour's Day, to scenes from the film Wilde (1997), starring Stephen Fry as Oscar Wilde. Dorset-born Arthur Evans Moule (1836–1918), a friend of novelist Thomas Hardy, wrote about Durdle Door in his 1879 book of poetry Songs of Heaven and Home, Written in a Foreign Land:

Shall the tide thus ebb and flow forever?

and for evermore

Rave the wave and glance the ripple through

the rocks at Durdle Door?

Durdle Door — iStock

Dorset Naga chilli
Creative Commons

The **Dorset Naga**, grown in Dorset, claims to be the hottest chilli in the world. Described as 'something only those with asbestos-lined stomachs should even consider trying', it has an average score of 923,000 Scoville Heat Units, almost twice the heat of the current Guinness World Record holder. It was created in 2008 by Joy and Michael Michaud at their home in West Bexington, near Dorchester, developed from a Bangladeshi pepper they bought at an Oriental food shop in Bournemouth. The Dorset Naga is so potent that handling it requires wearing gloves, and they need to be cut outside in a strong wind to avoid stinging the eyes. The couple run a business, Peppers by Post, and sold a quarter of a million of their chillies to customers worldwide in the first year alone.

On 12 July 1910 the co-founder of Rolls Royce, Charles Rolls, became **Britain's first air crash fatality.** A true aviation pioneer, Rolls had crossed the English Channel by balloon in 1906, and just a month before his fatal crash had made the first two-way aeroplane crossing of the Channel. He was an experienced pilot and had made more than 200 flights in his Wright Flyer. The accident that killed him happened at an air display in Hengistbury airfield, Southbourne, near Bournemouth, in front of a large crowd of spectators. It was caused by the tail of the plane breaking off, causing the craft to plunge rapidly to the ground.

Maiden Castle, the ancient earthwork fortress near Dorchester, was occupied from around 3500 BC until the arrival of the Romans in AD 43. For most of that time the site was apparently a camp, only fortified in about 350 BC. The defenders were serious about defence: excavations revealed a store of about 20,000 stones (from Chesil Beach) for use in slings! However, it appears that they were outsmarted as one of the skeletons discovered at the site was found to have a Roman catapult bolt in its spine.

St Mary's, in the grounds of Lulworth Castle, is a church that couldn't look like a church. It was built by Thomas Weld in 1795, when he received permission

St Mary's, Lulworth
Creative Commons

from King George III to erect the first Catholic church since the Reformation. The permission was granted only on condition that it did not look like a church; instead it was built to resemble a garden temple!

Painting of Robinson Crusoe by Walter Paget 1894

Poole Harbour is the second largest natural harbour in the world after Sydney, Australia. From here, in 1708, two small ships, the Duke and the Duchess, captained by Woodes Rogers, set sail to find treasure and adventures in the South Seas. But better than that, they achieved fame, for they found Robinson Crusoe. Swept far south by a storm off Cape Horn, they were forced to take shelter at a small island called Juan Fernandez and were amazed that night to see a light blazing on the shore. Captain Rogers sent out a boat, which returned with a scruffy, bearded man clothed in goatskins, who spoke English. The man was Alexander Selkirk, a sailor whose story was retold as Robinson Crusoe by Daniel Defoe.

And speaking of adventures on islands, Brownsea Island, which lies at the mouth of Poole Harbour, is where the world-famous **Boy Scout Movement** was born. It began in August 1907 when twenty boys, mostly from local Boys' Brigades, as well as some pupils from Eton and Harrow, pitched their tents and began to learn about practical skills and the concepts of fair play and good manners from Lieutenant-General Sir Robert Baden Powell. The island is now owned by the National Trust and has one of the UK's few red squirrel colonies.

Scout stone
Creative Commons

Brownsea Island
iStock

Cowpox to the rescue!

Worth Matravers, a remote and windswept village high above the ocean on the Purbeck Hills, is home to one of the oldest churches in Dorset, with a Saxon doorway and Norman arches. In the bleak churchyard, under a mossy stone, lie a simple farmer and his wife. With their courage and instinct, they did more to improve the life of ordinary people than any world leader or renowned politician. In 1774, farmer Benjamin Jesty was living at Yetminster, near Sherborne, an area ravaged by smallpox. With a pregnant wife and three small children to support, he was obviously worried for the health of his family. He noticed that his two dairymaids, both of whom had suffered from the mild complaint of cowpox, had nursed family members suffering from the more serious and highly contagious smallpox and yet neither of them had caught the disease themselves. From this observation, he concluded that cowpox gave immunity to smallpox.

Determined to give his wife and children a dose of cowpox, he took them to a nearby farm at Chetnole, where there was an outbreak of the infection. In an open field, he took some fluid from an infected cow and, using a knitting needle, scratched his wife's arm and injected the fluid, thus performing the world's first recorded vaccination. The term vaccination comes from the Latin word for cow, vacca. He then repeated the procedure on his two sons. All of them suffered for a few days with the cowpox and then recovered.

In 1797 the Jestys moved to Worth Matravers, where Benjamin performed many more vaccinations on the local people. On his gravestone are the words, 'the first person (known) that introduced the Cow Pox by inoculation'.

Jestys' gravestones
Creative Commons

'Bloody' history of Dorset!

On 11 June 1685 James Scott, 1st Duke of Monmouth, the pretender to the throne, landed on the beach at Lyme Regis with about eighty men, including England's first novelist, Daniel Defoe. They marched north, picking up support as they went and clashed with the forces of James II, led by John Churchill (later Duke of Marlborough), at Sedgemoor in Somerset on 6 July. Monmouth's army was badly defeated and he ran away across country with Lord Grey and three companions.

They headed to Dorset, where they hoped to catch a boat from Poole to Holland. At Woodyates, just inside Dorset to the north, was an inn owned by the Earl of Shaftesbury and run by Robert Browning, an ancestor of the poet. Here the group left their horses and split up, Monmouth disguised as a shepherd. He made his way into open country near Horton, and was spotted climbing over a hedge by an old woman living in a nearby cottage. A search was organised at sunrise and a soldier spotted what looked like a pile of clothes in a ditch underneath an ash tree. He pulled out the Duke of Monmouth, by then haggard and scruffy, with nothing in his pockets except raw peas and a badge of the Order of the Garter, given to him by his father, Charles II. The spot has been known ever since as Monmouth's Ash. Monmouth was beheaded on Tower Hill on 15 July. Afterwards, at the 'Bloody Assizes' of Judge Jeffreys, over 300 of Monmouth's supporters were executed. The defeat at Sedgemoor was not entirely unproductive for Daniel Defoe, however. While hiding in a churchyard during his escape, he saw the name Robinson Crusoe on a gravestone and filled it away for later use!

Smallest pub in the world

After the Restoration, Charles II returned many times to Dorset to thank those who had helped him during his escape after the Battle of Worcester in 1651. On one of these trips, he stopped in Godmanstone and asked at the blacksmith's for a glass of ale. The blacksmith replied that he was

Old Smith's Arms,
Godmanstone
Creative Commons

unable to oblige as he had no licence to sell alcohol. 'From now on, you have a licence to sell beer and porter,' announced the king, and the Old Smith's Arms at Godmanstone was born. At 20 feet (6m) by 10 feet (3m), it was thought to be the smallest public house in the world.

Saints and spies

The very ancient church of St Candida and St Cross in Whitchurch Canicorum is unique in that it is the only parish church in England containing the bones of its patron saint. The relics of St Wite (or Candida in Latin) are in a stone altar in which there are three openings (or healing holes) intended for the insertion of diseased limbs. A more modern martyr, Georgi Markov, lies in the same churchyard with English words on one side of his stone and Bulgarian on the other. 'Bulgaria's most revered dissident' was assassinated on Waterloo Bridge by a communist agent, using an air gun disguised as an umbrella to inject him with a pin-head-sized pellet of the lethal poison, ricin. That crime of the Cold War took place in September 1978.

Dorset's Hippocrates!

Wynford Eagle is the birthplace of hero of the Civil War and the father of English medicine, Thomas Sydenham, who was born in 1624 in the manor house which still stands in the village. Surprisingly, there is no memorial to this great British physician. Called the English Hippocrates, he revived the Hippocratic methods of observations and experience. For him the foundation of medicine was not scientific examination but bedside experience. He noted the link between fleas and typhus fever, introduced opium into medical practice, was the first to use iron in treating anaemia and quinine in treating malaria. His fame came mostly from the fact that he alleviated the suffering of the sick and made ill people well. He is also renowned for discovering the disease, Sydenham's chorea, also known as 'St Vitus Dance'.

CUSTOMS AND TRADITIONS

Tolpuddle Martyrs'
Festival
Creative Commons

Tolpuddle Martyrs' Festival

The Tolpuddle Martyrs' Festival is held annually in Tolpuddle, usually in the third week of July, organised by the Trades Union Congress (TUC). In the 1830s, life in villages like Tolpuddle was hard and getting worse. Farm workers couldn't bear any more cuts to their pay so some fought back by smashing the new agricultural machines, but this brought only harsh punishments.

In 1834, farm workers in west Dorset formed a trade union. Unions were legal and growing fast but six leaders of the union were arrested and sentenced to seven years' transportation (to Australia!) for taking an oath of secrecy. A massive protest swept across the country. Thousands of people marched through London and many more organised petitions and protest meetings to demand their freedom. The protest campaign proved successful and the Tolpuddle Martyrs returned home in triumph. The Tolpuddle story is about how ordinary working people combined together to defend their families.

Today the annual festival features a parade of banners from many trade unions, a memorial service, speeches and music. Recent festivals have featured speakers such as Tony Benn and musicians such as Billy Bragg, as well as local folk singers and others from all around the world.

Tolpuddle Martyrs' Festival banner
Creative Commons

Foodie facts ...

Wimborne St Giles is a handsome brick village near Cranborne and the ancient seat of the Earls of Shaftesbury. In the grand church, refashioned in the 18th century, is the imposing tomb of Sir Anthony Ashley. A strange ball carved on his tomb gives away his guilty secret, for Sir Anthony was the first man to introduce into England that green vegetable despised by children across the land, **the cabbage**. He brought it across from Holland and, in 1539, the first cabbage grown in England was cultivated in the kitchen garden of St Giles House, Wimborne St Giles. The ball on the tomb represents that very cabbage!

Dorset's favourite soup, however, is made not with cabbage but with lettuce. A recipe for **Studland Sea Lettuce Soup** uses a whole bucket of fresh sea lettuce, picked early in the morning from the tide line!

Alongside the traditional cream tea, Dorset has brought a splendid array of sweet recipes to English cuisine. The gooseberry is the star of **Blandford Pudding**, which comes from the market town of the same name, and is probably tastier than it sounds. **Dorset Apple Cake** is the favourite local dessert, and, as with many a regional delicacy, everyone has their own preferred recipe. However, most traditional recipes involve the 'rubbed-in' method, mixed with milk to produce a scone-like mixture, and most use diced cooking apples. Some add spices, eggs or butter.

Dorset's signature cheese is **Dorset Blue Vinny**, a hard, crumbly cheese, coloured creamy white with fine blue veins. The word Vinny comes from *vinew* or *fyne* in Old English – meaning 'mould'. Nowadays it's produced on Woodbridge Farm in Sturminster Newton by the Davies family, who revived a 300-year-old recipe in 1980. In times gone by, Dorset Blue Vinny was found in nearly every farmhouse in the county, and was a good way of using leftover milk after the cream had been skimmed off for making butter. Being skimmed, the cheese didn't 'blue' naturally. Instead, the mould had to be encouraged. This could be done by a number of interesting methods, from dipping old horse harnesses into the vats, to storing the cheese on damp stones covered with hessian sacks, or simply next to a pair of mouldy boots. Presumably today's methods are a tad more hygienic! One story relates that the rind of the Blue Vinny is so hard that a train once used it as replacement wheels.

Apples also go into **frumenty**, a kind of pottage made with boiled wheat, milk, eggs, and various fruits, which was often sold at travelling fairs. This dish was traditionally eaten on Mothering Sunday, when servants were permitted to visit their mothers, who would take advantage of the occasion to make sure their sons had a hearty meal. For centuries, frumenty was part of the Celtic Christmas meal. In fact, it's thought to be England's oldest national dish.

Golden Cap near Seatown, the highest point on the south coast, has a dessert named after it: **Golden Cap steamed pudding**, flavoured with marmalade to match the warm colour that gives the cliff top its name.

Golden Cap steamed pudding and Golden Cap, Seatown: spot the difference!
Creative Commons

Or why not try **Dorset Knobs** – crisp little roll-shaped biscuits made by Moores of Morcombelake, who have been baking biscuits in the county since before 1860. The Knobs are shaped by hand, baked at a high temperature and left in a low oven until completely dried out – the result is a wonderfully versatile rusk-like biscuit that can be spread with butter, eaten with cheese or soup, or dipped in tea.

WHAT'S IN A NAME?

The earliest recorded use of the name Dorset was in AD 940 as the Celtic 'Dorseteschire', meaning 'the place of fisticuffs'. It comes from *saete* ('dwellers') and *Dornuuarana* ('Dorchester'), which in turn derives from the Welsh dwrn meaning 'fist' and gwarae meaning 'play'.

Most Dorset place names have Old English or Anglo-Saxon origins. The oldest place names are Celtic – river names like Cerne, Char, Lim, Trent and Wey. Dorset also has more than its fair share of amusing place names, which provide quite a contrast to the often idyllic hamlets they refer to. Where else in the world would you find Droop, Dungy Head or Happy Bottom?

The Piddle Valley often gets a giggle, but *piddle* simply means 'marsh or fen', from the Old English word *pidele*. The valley takes its name from the River Piddle that runs through it, once called the Pidelen. Piddletrenthide, the first village to which the River Piddle gives its name, is described in the Domesday Book as an 'estate on the River Piddle assessed at thirty hides'. 'Trente' comes from the French *trente* for 'thirty', and 'hide' from an Old English term meaning 'a hide of land'.

As well as Piddletrenthide, the river has passed on its quirky name to many of the places it passes through. After Piddletrenthide and Piddlehinton, the villages on the Piddle are called Puddle: there's Puddletown, Tolpuddle, Affpuddle, Briantspuddle and Turnerspuddle. It was the Victorians who prudishly changed the spelling to 'puddle', though Puddletown got away with being called Piddletown into the 1950s. Walk the two-and-a-half-mile trail along the river from Piddlehinton to Piddletrenthide and you can even enjoy a Piddle Ale at the Piddle Inn there.

Piddle Inn Signs
Creative Commons

Old Harry and his Wife — iStock

The charming Scratchy Bottom is a clifftop valley in Lulworth, and lies between Durdle Door and Swyre Head. Its name is thought to refer to its rough and rugged surfaces!

Several places in Dorset tell old tales of the devil and his roguery – such as the Agglestone, a 400-ton sandstone rock perched on top of a hill about a mile away from Studland. *Agglestone* means 'Prince's Stone' in Old English. According to folklore, the massive stone was thrown by the devil – the 'Prince of Darkness' – all the way from the Isle of Wight in an attempt to demolish Corfe Castle.

Dewlish is an old Celtic name that means 'devilish' and is named after the stream that runs through the village, today called Devil's Brook. One of the devil's more affable nicknames, Old Harry, was bestowed upon the Old Harry Rocks in Studland during the 18th century. The main rock ('Harry') is about 40 feet tall (12.2 m), while the now-collapsed 'Wife' rock can only be seen at low tide. The chain of chalk rocks used to stretch from Purbeck to the Isle of Wight until the ice age and weathering damaged it. The similar but less dramatic structures on the Isle of Wight are called 'the Needles'.

Pokesdown was once called 'Pooksdown', as it was thought to be home to 'pucks' or mischievous sprites.

Grim's Ditch is one of many prehistoric earthworks in England to be named 'grim', a word the Anglo Saxons used to name features with unexplained origins. The name may come from the Old Norse word *grimr*, an alias for the Norse God of War and Magic, Odin, or 'the masked one'. Earthworks such as Grim's Ditch were possibly perceived as the mysterious work of Odin, or connected with worship of him. Since Odin is, among other things, a god of war, the Anglo-Saxons may have thought the earthworks were created by him and intended for military use.

Unfortunately for residents of Bleet Farm in Gillingham, the town's Old English namesake *bleet* means 'wretched or miserable'. Fortuneswell in Portland, on the other hand, has a name that means 'lucky well or spring'. The name was first recorded as 'Fortune's Well' in 1608 after the ancient well at the centre of the village, and may have originated from a belief in the fortune-telling power of its water.

The grim legacy of public execution looms large in the names of Dorset villages. It's thought that Three Legged Cross in Verwood is named after the gallows, which were sometimes called 'the three-legged mare'. Worgret, near Wareham, also means 'gallows', whose Old English name was *weargrod*. The gallows were generally placed in open spaces, as public executions were considered prime entertainment, and large crowds would come to watch the proceedings. Gallows were also placed at the meeting points of roads and along the approach to towns, so that the dead would be seen by passing travellers – for example, at Gallows Corner near Milborne St Andrew. Gallows Hill in Dorchester was one of the main sites for public executions; town plans from 1610 depict a gallows made with a crossbeam wide enough for multiple hangings, which must have made quite a show for the locals.

And we can't possibly end this section without mention of the wonderful Ryme Intrinseca. A village in the Blackmoor Vale and situated four miles south of Yeovil, it's the name that Poet Laureate John Betjeman used to begin his poem Dorset, but oddly enough he misspelt it! The 'Ryme' part refers to *rim*, meaning a place that's on the edge or border. The word intrinseca in Latin means that it's within the bounds, as opposed to the opposite, extrinseca. There used to be a manor called Ryme Extrinseca, but it's gone now. The village has a population of about 150, and even boasts its own brewery.

FAMOUS NAMES OF DORSET

The English Romantic poet **Percy Bysshe Shelley** (1792–1822) is buried in the Protestant Cemetery in Rome, but his heart lies in St Peter's Churchyard in Bournemouth. It found its way there long after Shelley drowned in 1822, when his boat went down in a storm off the coast of the Gulf of Spezia. His body washed ashore and was cremated on the beach – but the story goes that his heart refused to burn, and was saved from

Percy Bysshe Shelley
Creative Commons

the flames by his friend Edward Trelawney. He returned it to what seemed its rightful place – the hands of the poet's widow, **Mary Shelley** (1797–1851), author of *Frankenstein*.

In 1851, an ailing Mary moved with her son, Sir Percy Florence Shelley, to what is now known as Shelley Manor, a clifftop house at Boscombe, Bournemouth. However, she died just weeks before the family could take up residence there. The heart was found among her possessions, wrapped in a copy of *Adonais*, her husband's elegy to the poet John Keats. It was placed in a casket and brought to Boscombe, where it's said to have sat for several decades on a plinth beneath a burning candle. Only when Percy Florence Shelley died in 1899 was the heart finally laid to rest, next to Mary and their son, in the family plot at St Peter's.

Shelley Manor has been used as a school, an art college, a museum, and even as the headquarters of the Home Guard. It narrowly escaped demolition some years ago, thanks to campaigners, who saw it as a vital part of Bournemouth's heritage. The house now serves an important purpose in the area as a medical centre and pharmacy. The Shelley family's other legacy, the Shelley Theatre, built by Percy Florence Shelley, is also alive and well; it provided a suitably

Gothic backdrop for productions of Mary Shelley's Frankenstein in 2010, performed by candlelight when the building was still only half-refurbished.

Adored children's author **Enid Blyton** (1897–1968) became fond of Dorset from her first visit in 1931, and used it to create a landscape of seashores, smugglers' tunnels and windy clifftops for the young heroes of her *Famous Five* stories. She visited Swanage in 1940 and took the steam train to Corfe Castle, a journey which is thought to have inspired her first Famous Five book *Five on a Treasure Island* (1942). Over the next twenty years, she returned often, staying at The Ship, The Grosvenor and The Grand Hotels in Swanage and swimming around what were two piers at the Peveril end of Swanage Bay. In 1950, she and her husband Kenneth bought Purbeck Golf Club for £1!

Many of the *Famous Five* books tell stories of the children exploring the area around the Isle of Purbeck and Poole Harbour. Brownsea Island provides the spooky setting for several of the Five's adventures. 'Whispering Island', as it sometimes appears in the stories, is now managed by the National Trust. But in Enid

Blyton's day, it was owned by the reclusive Mrs Bonham-Christie, whose dislike of visitors and insistence on leaving the island in its natural state inspired Enid to name it 'Keep Away Island'. Stoborough Heath, between Stoborough and Corfe, reappears as 'Mystery Moor', while Corfe Castle itself becomes 'Kirrin Castle'. 'Finniston Farm' is based on Enid's own farm at Sturminster Newton.

Five on a Treasure Island, Enid Blyton Creative Commons

In 1949, the author first introduced one of her best-loved children's characters in *Little Noddy Goes to Toyland*. Noddy's home of Toytown was based on the village of Studland, with its quaint cottages and soft, sandy beach. The local bobby in Toytown, Mr Plod, was inspired by a real Dorset officer, PC Christopher Rhone, whom Enid would have met as he went about his beat in Studland.

Gold Hill in Shaftesbury was immortalised by Hovis bread in 1973, in what has been voted Britain's all-time favourite television advertisement. A delivery boy is seen pushing his bike, the basket full of fresh loaves, up a cobbled street so steep that it's like 'taking bread to the top of the world' – then whizzing joyfully down again. The view from the top of the street, lined with thatched cottages and overlooking the Blackmore Vale, is held to be one of England's most romantic sights, and can be spotted on the covers of numerous books about rural England, as well as on chocolate boxes and calendars. Still commonly known as 'Hovis Hill', it also appears in the 1967 film version of Thomas Hardy's *Far From the Madding Crowd*.

Gold Hill, Shaftesbury — iStock

The vast majority of '**Hardy Country**' or 'Hardy's Wessex' – a 'landscape of the mind' in which the English novelist Thomas Hardy set his tales – is based on places around Dorset and Hardy's own life there. He was born in a thatched cottage in Higher Bockhampton – which in his novels became Upper Mellstock – in 1840, and christened at the church at Stinsford, where his first wife Emma is now buried. He wanted to be buried with her, but he lies instead in Poet's Corner in Westminster Abbey. Only his heart lies in Emma's grave – well, most of it, at least: it is reported that the doctor who removed the heart was called away momentarily and returned to find his cat had begun to eat it!

Hardy's cousin Tryphena Sparks, the inspiration for his poem *Thoughts of Phena at News of Her Death* (1890), was a resident of Puddletown, as were his grandfather and great-grandfather. This village was Hardy's model for Weatherbury, the central setting for *Far from the Madding Crowd* (1874). The heroine Bathsheba's farmhouse has been linked with Waterston Manor, a late-16th-century structure which stands just off the B3142; and the porch of St Mary's Church is the same one under which Troy falls asleep, after an evening spent tirelessly planting flowers around the recently deceased Fanny's tomb. The shepherd Gabriel Oak loses his flock on 'Norcombe', which is Toller Down just north of Bridport – an incident which foreshadowed the threat to the Dorset farming industry in the mid-19th century, when steamships made possible the importation of New Zealand lambs.

The novel's title is taken from a line in Thomas Gray's *Elegy Written in a Country Churchyard* (1751): 'Far from the madding crowd's ignoble strife, their sober wishes never learned to stray.' It was a notion that would have appealed to many at a time when more and more Victorian readers sought to escape the drab cities by way of romantic tales of rural life. Hardy's stories follow in the tradition of old country ballads, this one in particular a tale of a proud beauty courted by a shepherd, a farmer and a dashing soldier.

The town of Bere Regis features in the same novel and in *Tess of the d'Urbervilles* (1891), which follows an ill-fated woman in her adventures and misadventures across Dorset. The Turbervilles were a real family, whose coat of arms is on display in Bere Regis Church and whose tombs surround it. They acquired the church in the 13th century and owned it for nearly 500 years. Tess's father,

John Durbeyfield, alludes to them when he says, 'Under the church of that there parish lie my ancestors – hundreds of 'em – in coats of mail and jewels.'

'He jumped up from his seat ... and went quickly toward the desire of his eyes.'
1891 illustration of Tess of the D'Urbervilles, by Joseph Syddall

Hardy's home for most of his life was Max Gate, a town house he designed himself in 1885 and named after a local tollgate keeper. Here you'll find the grave of the author's dog, aptly named Wessex.

T.E. Lawrence (1888–1935), better known as Lawrence of Arabia, once lived in Bovington in a tiny cottage called Clouds Hill. He was born in Caernarfonshire in Wales, and in the years leading up to the First World War studied history at Oxford University. He went on to work and travel as an archaeologist in the Middle East, notably in Syria and what was then Palestine. There he got to know the Arabs and the lands they lived in, learning their languages and reading about their history. In 1914, he joined the army and gained a reputation as a brilliant tactician during the Arab Revolt, helping the Arabs to achieve military success and a chance at self-government.

Lawrence in Arabia, 1919, taken by Lowell Thomas (University of Toronto)

However, Lawrence became disillusioned by defeats and felt he had not kept his promises to the Arabs. He turned down a series of high honours and enlisted in the RAF as an aircraftsman – a position far beneath him – under a false name, to escape a celebrity he had acquired quite by accident.

When the press discovered him again, he hid in the Tank Corps at Bovington and assumed the name T.E. Shaw. It was then that Clouds Hill provided him with a place to which to retreat and write. He rented and later bought it from the Framptons, cousins of his who owned Bovington Camp, and saved the tiny cottage from ruin, re-roofing it, installing a bathroom and decorating it meticulously. Here he was able to retire from the limelight and concentrate on finishing his book about his Arabian adventures, *The Seven Pillars of Wisdom*. He was also able to indulge his passion for motorbikes, and was often to be seen speeding around the Dorset lanes. In May 1935, he rode his Brough Superior to Bovington Camp, to send a telegraph, and then set out on the return journey, along the straight stretch of road to Clouds Hill. He had just crested a slight rise when he swerved to avoid two errand boys on bicycles and was knocked unconscious. He remained in a coma for several days and died on 19 May, aged only 46. Many dignitaries attended his burial, including the King of Iraq. A tree was planted to mark the site of the accident and the T.E. Lawrence Society has now added a stone memorial. Decades after his death, conspiracy theorists still speculate that his death had been an assassination, and some believe it still.

Most of the existing poetry written in the Dorset dialect is the work of **William Barnes** (1801–86), 'the Dorsetshire Poet' or 'the People's Poet', who was born in Blackmore Vale to farm workers. Like many poets who wrote in their regional dialects, William was truly part of his community, and poetry was not his sole profession – he was at various times a lawyer's clerk, a schoolteacher, a clergyman and a scholar proficient in 70 languages. He was ordained in 1847 and became rector of Winterborne Came, near Dorchester, in 1862, where he lived for the rest of his life. He'd been writing poetry since 1833, recording the lives of rural folk in their own language. *Poems of Rural Life in the Dorset Dialect* was published in 1844, *Hwomely Rhymes* in 1857, and a third volume in 1863. Although he produced one volume in Standard English, it was never reprinted, and Barnes always seemed more in his element in the dialect he'd heard his parents speaking as a boy. He wrote in the preface to his first collection that he considered dialect to be the most natural form of expression: 'It is my mother's tongue, and to my mind, the only true speech of the life that I draw.'

Zummer an' Winter by **William Barnes**

When I led by zummer streams

The pride o' Lea, as naighbours thought her,

While the zun, wi' evenen beams,

Did cast our sheades athirt the water;

Winds a-blowen,

Streams a-flowen,

Skies a-glowen,

Tokens ov my jay zoo fleeten,

Heightened it, that happy meeten.

Then, when maid an' man took pleaces,

Gay in winter's Chris'mas dances,

Showen in their merry feaces

Kindly smiles an' glisnen glances;

Stars a-winken,

Day a-shrinken,

Sheades a-zinken,

Brought anew the happy meeten,

That did meake the night too fleeten.

The **Cerne Abbas Giant**, otherwise known as 'The Rude Man' because of his obvious virility, is one of the largest hill figures in Britain at 180 feet (55m) tall, holding aloft a huge knobbed club 120 feet (37m) long. His striking figure is formed by a trench a foot wide and a foot deep, cut into the chalky ground. He is one of only two surviving hill figures in Britain that represent the human form, the other being the Long Man of Wilmington in East Sussex.

The earliest written record of the Giant dates back to 1751 in a letter by John Hutchins, a Dorset historian, who seems to think the figure was carved in the mid-1600s. It seems unlikely that the residents of the nearby Cerne Abbey would have tolerated the pagan fertility symbol for very long, which has led some to put his origins at somewhere in the mid-17th century. However, the style of the drawing, and the Iron Age earthwork close by, suggests much earlier origins.

Cerne Abbas Giant
Creative Commons

It's likely he was made to depict the Greek and Roman god of strength, Hercules, who traditionally carried a club. The worship of Hercules may have arrived in the early part of the Roman invasion, and then become mingled with a similar god of a local Celtic tribe. Most historians believe the Giant was probably cut during the reign of the Emperor Commodus (AD 180–93). Commodus was so proud of his own physical prowess as to believe himself a reincarnation of Hercules, and is known to have ordered numerous statues depicting himself as the divine hero.

Or could the Rude Man have been the work of some mischievous monks from the nearby abbey? One story relates that the figure was cut by the monks as a practical joke on their abbot, Thomas Corton. Another local legend describes the figure as the remnants of a real Danish giant who descended on the English coast, leading an invasion of the country. He unwittingly fell asleep on the hillside and the locals seized their chance to fight back, cutting off his head as he slept. They then drew around his figure to mark the place where he met his end, perhaps to deter any future gargantuan invaders.

Today, the Giant is kept in good shape and free from grass by scouring every few years, and in 2013 even wore a fashionable grass moustache in support of 'Movember', where men grow moustaches throughout the month of November to raises awareness of prostate and testicular cancer – a most fitting cause for our Cerne Giant!

The poet **Cecil Day-Lewis** was buried in 1972 in St Michael's Churchyard, Stinsford. Also buried here are Thomas Hardy's heart and his two wives. Day-Lewis's poetry was much influenced by Hardy and that's what led to his desire to be buried near him. Day-Lewis was educated at Sherborne and Wadham College, Oxford, where he encountered W.H. Auden and became part of a group of left-wing poets. In 1951, he was appointed Professor of Poetry at Oxford and, in 1968, he became Poet Laureate after the death of John Masefield. Day-Lewis was a renowned womaniser and had extramarital affairs with a number of women, including the model Jane Howard. The actor Daniel Day-Lewis is his son by his second wife, Jill Balcon. Later in life, he became an increasingly public figure, sitting on many committees, delivering lectures and making broadcasts. Today, however, his work is not held in the same regard as that of Auden, and he was refused a plaque in 'Poets' Corner' in Westminster Abbey.

Other famous sons and daughters of Dorset include musician **PJ Harvey**, who was born and grew up on a farm near Bridport and was recently awarded an MBE for her services to music, and comedian **Alan Carr**, who was born in Weymouth. Celebrities who have made Dorset their home include the creator of Downton Abbey, **Julian Fellows**; world-famous investigative journalist **Kate Adie**; **Billy Bragg**, singer and songwriter and left-wing activist; and **Ian Gillan**, front man of the famous rock band Deep Purple.

Downton Abbey the cast

Tony Hancock, one of Britain's best-known comedians and actors, was brought up in Bournemouth, where his father worked as an entertainer at the Railway Hotel in Holdenhurst Road. He was educated at Durlston Court, but left school at 15. His popular show *Hancock's Half Hour* is now a British comedy classic. The Oscar-winning actor and star of *The Dark Knight* and *American Psycho*, **Christian Bale**, attended Bournemouth School until the age of 16, making his film debut aged just 13 in Steven Spielberg's *Empire of the Sun*. He earned a reputation as a method actor after he lost 63 pounds for his role in *The Machinist*. Legendary creator of Middle Earth, **J.R.R. Tolkien**, spent the final part of his life in Bournemouth, accompanied by his wife Edith. He'd previously come on holiday to the seaside town every summer for thirty years, always staying at the same room in the Hotel Miramar. He lived in a house off Branksome Chine from the 1960s until his death in 1973.

MISCELLANEOUS

Granny's Teeth

In Lyme Regis, the prominent stone steps on the famous breakwater The Cobb, known as Granny's Teeth, are where Jane Austen's character Louisa Musgrove flirts with Captain Wentworth in Persuasion, and jumps down the steps, before running back up them and jumping down when 'she fell on the pavement on the Lower Cobb, and was taken up lifeless!' Anyone who has used Granny's Teeth to ascend from the Lower Cobb, or worse yet, gone down them, knows that running – either up or down them – would be a crazy exercise. In 1980, Meryl Streep starred in *The French Lieutenant's Woman*, which was filmed mainly in Lyme Regis. The most enduring image is of Streep dressed in a black cloak standing on the breakwater of The Cobb.

Visitors cautiously descending Granny's Teeth on The Cobb at Lyme Regis — iStock

Ancient astronomical clock

The famous clock at Wimborne Minster was built in about 1320 – long before man appreciated the fact that the earth moves round the sun, rather than the other way round! As a consequence, the earth is in the centre and the sun, moon and stars all revolve around the outside. The sun in the outer circle represents the hour hand, the moon represents the phases of the lunar month, and the earth is fixed. It's a 24-hour clock and is still accurate after almost seven centuries. It was made by Peter Lightfoot, a monk from Glastonbury Abbey.

Astronomical Clock, Wimborne Minster
Creative Commons

Grass staircase

This staircase, which can be found in Milton Abbey park and gardens, comprises 111 steps of turf between two yew hedges. At the top of the steps is a chapel originally built by the Saxons and then rebuilt in the 12th century by the Normans. The story goes

Grass staircase
Creative Commons

that the chapel, dedicated to St Catherine, is on the very spot where Athelstan, first King of all England, camped with his guards on their journey north to meet the Danes, and he dreamt he would win. The dream came true and Athelstan founded Milton Abbey in thanks.

The oldest letter box in the UK

Made by John N Butt and Co. of Gloucester between 1853 and 1856, the pillar box in Holwell is the oldest still in use in Great Britain. Although made of metal and painted red, it's quite different to the ones we see today. Firstly, it's octagonal instead of circular, and has the words 'Post Office Letterbox' cast at the top, above the cipher of Queen Victoria and the maker's name. The slot for the letters is very small and is vertical rather than horizontal, and a swinging flap on the inside of the hole keeps out the rain!

Post box, Holwell
Creative Commons

Red signpost

Until quite recently even the authorities who paint this signpost red at regular intervals didn't know why! There have long been legends of murder and hangings, but the real reason is as strange as any of those legends. If at the Red Signpost you turn down the lane to Bloxworth, after about 100 yards you'll reach Botany Bay Farm. In it is a half-destroyed barn built like a prison with narrow slits for windows. Constructed in the late 18th century, the barn was used to house prisoners who had been condemned at Dorchester to transportation to Australia. The prisoners would have to walk to Portsmouth to get on the boat, and Botany Bay Farm was the first night's stop, being 14 miles from Dorchester. In those days, most

Red signpost
Creative Commons

people couldn't read, including the guards, and the red post was a sign for them to turn off with the prisoners for a night's lodging!

Where the Stars and Stripes began

In the beautiful hamlet of Steeple, which consists of a church, a farmhouse and a manor house can be found the origins of the USA's flag – the Stars and Stripes. Cut in stone in the porch of the church is a coat of arms, which is repeated in scarlet paint on the barrel roof. It's the coat of arms of the Lawrences, a family allied to George Washington's ancestors. George Washington wore their arms on his signet ring, and when he came to design a flag for the newly formed United States, he used the arms showing the Stars and Stripes to be seen in this small church.

Buried in his own dining table

On the south chancel wall in the parish church at Charmouth there is a memorial to the Rev. Edward Bragge, who died in

1747. The clergyman was a great gourmet, so much so that when he was dying he told his friends that he wanted to be buried in the table at which he'd eaten so many good meals throughout his life. His friends honoured his wish by cutting up the table and turning it into a coffin, which was duly buried at the church!

BOOK ENDS

Here are some more random, but brief, facts about Dorset that I believe warrant a mention – mainly trivia but some are tales!

1. **Poole Harbour** is the largest natural harbour in Britain. It was formed at the end of the last Ice Age when what was a valley was filled by rising seas.

2. **Sandbanks** in Poole is the most expensive place to live in Europe. Even during the financial crisis one plot was advertised in 2009 for roughly £10,000 per square metre!

3. Many of the questions for the original Trivial Pursuit game were researched in the public library in Weymouth.

4. On Weymouth Beach, George III became the first monarch to use a bathing machine. His health was not very robust and in 1788

he suffered his first attack of porphyria. Recovering from this bout of illness, he made his first visit to Weymouth in 1789. The benefits of the salt water of the sea were being praised by the doctors of the day. Using the bathing machine, George took a dip in the bay; the machines were designed as mobile changing rooms and could be wheeled into the water to allow discreet entry into the sea. As George emerged from the water, a band played God Save the King.

5. David Cornwell, better known as the author John le Carré, was born in Poole in 1931.

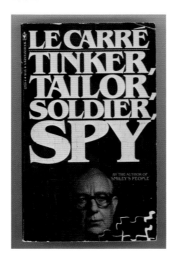

Tinker, Tailor, Soldier, Spy, by John Le Carré
Creative Commons

6. The man who inspired Shakespeare to write The Tempest lies buried at Whitchurch Canonicorum. Sir George Somers was a man of great energy: not only did he sail with Sir Walter Raleigh and capture treasure ships, but he was also Mayor of Lyme Regis (where he was born) and found time to become a Member of Parliament. He is best known for his colonisation of Virginia and Bermuda.

7. RAF pilots wiggle their wings when flying over the lime trees in Parnham Park, Beaminster. This is in memory of two hero airmen – a father and his son – who are buried beneath the trees.

8. Naturists can enjoy 800 metres of seashore along the coast at Studland, considered to be one of the best nudist beaches in the country.

9. On a vaguely similar note, naked rambler Stephen Gough from Bournemouth was

arrested 15 times on his walk from Land's End to John O'Groats in 2003, when he wore nothing more than socks and shoes, a rucksack and a hat!

10.Hitler's desk can be found in the Dorset Regiment Museum in Dorchester.

11.Little Green Men are to be found in many churches in Dorset: Child Okeford, Cattistock, Bere Regis, Mappowder, Iwerne Minster, Winterborne Whitechurch and Sherborne Abbey. They're not of the alien variety, however, but are leafy faces carved into various nooks and crannies – relics of old pagan tree-worship.

12.The famous film, The African Queen, starring Humphrey Bogart and Katharine Hepburn, was partly filmed in Dorset. In some scenes, the river used is not the 2,900-mile Congo but Dorset's somewhat shorter River Piddle!

13. Expectant seahorses spotted in the ocean at Studland indicate that there was a baby boom in 2008! Conservationists are worried that too much boating activity might destroy them and so have asked boat owners to avoid any areas where eelgrass grows – the favourite habitat of the seahorses.

14. In 2007 the largest Bronze Age axe hoard to be found in Europe was discovered behind Putlake Farm, near Swanage.

15. The Martyrs' Tree in Tolpuddle is the largest sycamore in Dorset.

16. The Peace Garden at Affpuddle was given to the church by Sir Ernest Debenham, whose family founded the famous department stores.

17.In Colin Dexter's 1992 *The Way Through the Woods* Inspector Morse stayed at the Bay Hotel in Lyme Regis, which Dexter described to the Daily Telegraph as being heaven on earth.'I remember,'Dexter told the Telegraph, 'telling my publisher to turn to that section because I thought it was the best bit in the book, and the dear girl said she agreed with me but then suggested I leave it out"and got on with the story". That rather saddened me – but I didn't take any notice!'

18.Broadchurch, the acclaimed UK television drama, was set in West Bay, Bridport. The series starred David Tennant and Olivia Coleman, was nominated for seven BAFTA awards, and won Best Drama Series, Best Actress (Coleman) and Best Supporting Actor (David Bradley).

19.The Cenotaph, St Paul's Cathedral and Buckingham Palace are all made of Portland Stone quarried on the Isle of Portland.

St Paul's Cathedral — iStock

20. As an inquisitive teenager, Dorset's most famous author, Thomas Hardy, climbed a tree in front of Dorchester Prison to get a bird's eye view of the public hanging of Martha Brown, a servant accused of murdering her husband.

21. The annual World Nettle-Eating Championships, which take place at the Bottle Inn in Marshwood, began in 1986 as a result of a frivolous bet between two farmers regarding which of them had the longest stinging nettles in their fields!

22. The Saxon King Edward was murdered, aged 15, in Dorset in 978. It was believed to be on the orders of his step-mother, Elfrida, when he went to visit her at Corfe Castle. And the reason put forward was that she wanted her own son Ethelred (the Unready) to have the throne.

23. The last silk farm in Britain was Lullingstone Silk Farm near Sherborne, which once bred between three and four million silkworms a year!

24. Dorset lies above Europe's largest onshore oilfield! At its peak in the 1990s it was producing 110,000 barrels a day. The area also contains an estimated 4.73 million tonnes of natural gas liquids and 1.42 billion cubic metres of natural gas.

25. Sir Winston Churchill was almost killed after falling from a bridge in Alum Chine, Bournemouth. While playing with his cousins he tried to leap from the bridge to a nearby tree but missed. He fell and was unconscious for three days. Thank goodness he recovered!

Other books in the Bradwell Books Tales & Trivia series

Available Now

Wiltshire Tales & Trivia

Hampshire Tales & Trivia

Somerset Tales & Trivia

Other titles for these counties include

Hampshire

Hampshire Dialect

Bradwell's Eclectica Hampshire

Bradwell's Eclectica Southampton

Hampshire Ghost Stories

Hampshire Wit & Humour

Walks for all Ages Hampshire *out in 2016*

Legends & Folklore Hampshire *out 2016*

Dorset

Walks for all Ages Dorset

Dorset Ghost Stories

Dorset Wit & Humour

Dorset Dialect

Legends & Folklore Dorset *out 2016*

Wiltshire

Wiltshire Dialect

Wiltshire Ghost Stories

Wiltshire Legends & Folklore

Walks for all Ages Wiltshire

Wiltshire Wit & Humour

Somerset

Somerset Dialect

Somerset Ghost Stories

Somerset Wit & Humour

Walks for all Ages Somerset

Walks for all Ages Exmoor

Legends & Folklore Somerset *out 2016*

For more details of these books
and other books you may be
interested in,visit
www.bradwellbooks.com

BIBLIOGRAPHY

David Hilliam, The Little Book of Dorset, The History Press, 2010

George Osborn, Dorset Curiosities, Dovecote Press Paperbacks, 1989

Peter Stanier, Shire County Guide: Dorset, Shire Publications 1986

Christopher Winn, I Never Knew That About England, Random House Group, 2008

Websites accessed April–May 2015

www.information-britain.co.uk/countydidyouknow.php?county=27

www.ruralview.co.uk/rural-views/5-interesting-facts-about-dorset

www.laverstockfarm.co.uk/well-i-never-knew-this-about-dorset/

www.sykescottages.co.uk/blog/dorsetsomerset/five-facts-about-dorset-9537

www.information-britain.co.uk/countydidyouknow.php?county=27

www.ruralview.co.uk/rural-views/5-interesting-facts-about-dorset

www.funkidslive.com/take-me-out/attractions/things-to-do-around-the-uk/dorset/

www.gov.uk/government/news/dorset-county-honoured-as-flag-flies-over-government

en.wikipedia.org/wiki/Abbotsbury_Swannery

en.wikipedia.org/wiki/River_Piddle

www.pri.org/stories/2013-08-19/piddle-or-puddle-curious-little-english-river

en.wikipedia.org/wiki/Scratchy_Bottom

www.portlandhistory.co.uk/fortuneswell.html

www.dorsetshire.com/poets.html

www.william-barnes-society.org.uk/p/literature.html

www.soas.ac.uk/research/rsa/journalofgraduateresearch/edition-5/file84475.pdf

www.darkdorset.co.uk/cerne_giant

www.bbc.co.uk/news/uk-england-dorset-24772626

www.opcdorset.org/FleetFiles/FleetJamesCrackerUFOs.htm

www.poetsgraves.co.uk/shelley.htm

en.wikipedia.org/wiki/Percy_Bysshe_Shelley#Shelley.27s_heart

www.historyinanhour.com/2013/07/08/the-death-of-percy-bysshe-shelley/

www.dorsetmagazine.co.uk/people/frankenstein_lives_mary_shelley_in_dorset_1_1640727

www.isleofpurbeck.com/blyton.html

www.policemag.co.uk/editions/nov13_VFTS.aspx

en.wikipedia.org/wiki/Gold_Hill,_Shaftesbury

www.britainexpress.com/History/bio/hardy-tours.htm

en.wikipedia.org/wiki/Puddletown

www.dorsetlife.co.uk/2008/09/a-dorset-love-story/

www.greatenglishchurches.co.uk/html/bere_regis.html

www.nationaltrust.org.uk/max-gate/

www.thebluevinny.co.uk/cheese.html

en.wikipedia.org/wiki/Mary_Anning

www.dinnerisserved1972.com/2013/01/07/golden-cap-pudding/

www.dorsetlife.co.uk/2009/11/dorset%E2%80%99s-plague-port/

en.wikipedia.org/wiki/Durdle_Door#In_literature_and_popular_culture

www.nationaltrust.org.uk/studland-beach/eating-and-shopping/article-1355778825535/

en.wikipedia.org/wiki/Frumenty

www.moores-biscuits.co.uk/aboutus.html

www.britannia.com/cooking/articles/dorset.html

www.englishtowncrier.co.uk/history.html#

www.poemhunter.com/poem/zummer-an-winter/#content

www.tolpuddlemartyrs.org.uk/

www.waymarking.com/waymarks/WMD9MV_The_Red_Post_
Botany_Bay_Farm_A31_Nr_Bloxworth_Dorset_UK